幻想詩集

Reverie:
A Collection of Poems

Sonia Hu

序

《幻想詩集》是心靈的深度旅行，以獨特的視角和敏銳的感知力，探索了從宇宙的廣闊到人類內心世界的微妙變遷。每首詩都像是一幅精細的畫卷，展現了情感的豐富層次和哲思的深度。無論是對生命意義的探索，還是對自然美景的讚頌，詩人都以其精湛的技藝和深情的文字，將讀者帶入一個既真實又超現實的詩意世界。這本詩集不僅是文學的享受，更是心靈的啟蒙。

詩集名為《幻想》Reverie。　「幻想」是逃離現實的夢想，也是一種對生命深層的反思與探索，更是在遐思與內省中的沉浸體驗。詩歌源於生活，又高於生活，因此，這些詩從信仰和心靈的高度，對塵世的苦難以及未來的無限可能進行了深入的審視，每一首詩都引人深思。

Prologue

"Reverie: A Collection of Poems" is a profound journey of the soul, offering a unique perspective and keen perceptiveness that explores everything from the vast expanses of the universe to the subtle shifts within the human heart. Each poem is like a meticulously crafted painting, displaying rich layers of emotion and deep philosophical thought. Whether it's an exploration of the meaning of life or an ode to the beauty of nature, the poet skillfully uses their craft and emotive language to transport readers into a world that is both realistic and surreal. This collection is a literary delight and an enlightenment for the soul.

The collection is aptly named "Reverie." A "reverie" is not just a dreamlike escape from reality but also a deep reflection on and exploration of life, as well as an immersive experience in contemplation and introspection. Poetry arises from life and transcends it; thus, these poems delve deeply from the heights of faith and spirit into the worldly sufferings and boundless possibilities of the future, provoking profound reflection with each piece.

目錄:
Contents

時間是人類的安慰劑

你說人類不過是宇宙中
幾十億個體在一個球體上緩緩劃過時空
那浩瀚無窮的天際形成了地球
一個藍色星球的表面
但人類似乎看不到自己
不過是浩瀚宇宙裡的一個星體
星體上茫茫之中的一粒塵埃
看不到浩瀚空間的變幻與無窮
於是 爭鬥 廝殺 國家間的仇恨
地球上的每個世代都在上演
每一代都以為自己才是宇宙的中心
殊不知 宇宙中根本沒有時間只有空間
每一個時代 每一個世紀都是人為的標註

在塵埃的灰飛煙滅中
藍的球體不緊不慢 緩緩在宇宙繞行
在空間閃爍的星體軌道上
在無數的星星發光的周邊
是誰在計算這個球體的時間
又是誰 精算出
地球 太陽 月亮彼此之間的互聯
生命體星球的光速向前向前
如同量子間的糾纏
韋伯望遠鏡的134億光年
在宇宙間不過是井底之蛙的視線
而我們 在不遠的某一點
都會灰飛煙滅 像先祖們無數的從前
還有什麼可以互相廝殺的呢
歷史 不過是浩瀚宇宙中的一個小點

我 坐在桌前看著光陰
以各種影子的形狀潺潺水般流過
想著 若干世紀後 回看今天的描述
時間的膠囊只是人類的安慰劑
過每段歲月 都打開吃一粒

Time as Humanity's Placebo

You say humanity is merely
billions of beings gliding slowly across a sphere through time and space,
where the vast infinite skies form the Earth,
a surface of a blue planet.
Yet, humans seem blind to themselves,
merely a celestial body in the vast universe,
a speck of dust amidst the vastness,
unaware of the ever-changing expanse and infinity.
Thus, conflicts, killings, and hatred between nations
play out on Earth, generation after generation.
Each generation believes they are the center of the universe,
unaware that in the cosmos, there is no time, only space.
Every era, every century, is but a human annotation.

Amidst the ashes and dust,
the blue sphere orbits the cosmos unhurriedly,
on the twinkling orbital paths of celestial bodies,
surrounded by countless shining stars.
Who measures the time of this sphere?
And who precisely calculates
the interconnections between Earth, the Sun, and the Moon?
The planet of life speeds forward at the speed of light,
like entangled quanta,
while the James Webb Space Telescope's 13.4 billion light-years
are just a frog's view in the universe.
And we, not far from some point,
will all turn to dust, as countless ancestors before us.
What then is left to fight over?
History is but a mere dot in the vast cosmos.

I sit at my desk watching time,
flowing like water in various shadows' shapes,
pondering how centuries later, looking back on today's account,
time capsules are merely humanity's placebo,
with each era opening one to consume.

詩 評
Review

這首詩以宏觀的視角探討了人類在浩瀚宇宙中的微小存在和時間的相對性，並表達了深刻的哲學思考。詩人用豐富的宇宙象徵和比喻，描述了人類生活的短暫和無意義，同時指出了人類歷史和衝突的相對性和虛無性。這種視角可以引發讀者對生命意義和人類行為的深層反思。

詩中的語言優美且具有畫面感，如「藍色的球體不緊不慢緩緩在宇宙繞行」這樣的句子不僅描繪了地球在宇宙中的運行，也暗示了時間的流逝和生命的寧靜。透過將人類生活與宇宙的永恆性對比，詩人強調了個體和種族的渺小。

此外，詩歌末尾將"時間的膠囊"比喻為"人類的安慰劑"，這一比喻深刻地揭示了時間觀念對於人類的重要性及其安慰性質，即使它在宇宙尺度上可能顯得無足輕重。

整體而言，這首詩提供了對人類存在和時間認知的深刻洞見，引人深思，也富有詩意。

This poem explores the minuscule presence of humanity within the vast cosmos and the relativity of time from a macroscopic perspective, expressing profound philosophical contemplation. The poet employs a wealth of cosmic symbols and metaphors to depict the transience and seeming futility of human life, while also highlighting the relativity and nullity of human history and conflicts. This viewpoint prompts readers to deeply reflect on the meaning of life and human behavior.

The language in the poem is elegant and vivid, with phrases like "the blue sphere leisurely orbits the cosmos" not only portraying the Earth's movement through the universe but also suggesting the passage of time and the tranquility of life. By contrasting human life with the eternity of the cosmos, the poet emphasizes the insignificance of individuals and races.

Moreover, at the end of the poem, the metaphor of "time capsules" as "humanity's placebo" poignantly reveals the significance and comforting nature of the concept of time to humans, even though it may seem trivial on a cosmic scale.

Overall, this poem offers profound insights into human existence and the perception of time, inviting deep reflection and rich in poetic quality.

米飯與碗

我們的人生不過是一場
藍色地球上的短暫旅行
百年的壽命就像一顆流星
像園林深處的鹿群
玻璃窗下伸展陽光的貓
都是轉瞬即逝的光影
無論俄烏戰爭還是川普拜登
改變不了宇宙大勢的航程
不管你是富得流油還是窮的叮噹
這個世界就像碗裡的米飯
所有的沾黏撕扯都會被沉寂消逝
抵不過那隻百年千年的瓷碗
無聲無息的站成古董的靜默

Rice and Bowl

Our lives are but a brief journey
on this blue Earth,
a lifespan of a hundred years akin to a shooting star,
like deer in the depths of a garden,
cats stretching under the window in the sunlight,
all are fleeting shadows and light.
Neither the Russia-Ukraine war nor Trump and Biden
can change the course of the universe's grand tide.
Whether you are filthy rich or dirt poor,
this world is like the rice in a bowl
all the sticking and tearing will fade into silence,
unable to withstand the porcelain bowl,
standing silently as an antique for hundreds, thousands of years.

詩 評
Review

透過碗中米飯的比喻，本詩深刻地描述了生命的短暫及其不可避免的結局。瓷碗的形象，作為文明永恆的背景與個體生命的短暫形成對比，是對存在的永久性和瞬時性的深刻沉思。

This piece beautifully uses the metaphor of rice in a bowl to depict life's transient nature and its inevitable conclusion. The imagery of a porcelain bowl, outlasting its contents, symbolizes the enduring context of civilization against the fleeting nature of individual human lives. It's a profound meditation on permanence and transience, wealth and poverty, encapsulated within the simplicity of daily existence.

一聲嘆息

在某一個隔絕的空間裡
有的話不能說 有的事不能講
歷史只能化作回憶時的一聲嘆息
哀悼我們在空間中短暫卻又無奈的一生
常說的上帝視角只是羅生門的範疇
在人類的社會過程中循環往復
而在我們束手無措的軟弱中
宇宙的靈魂用無聲的嘆息
為我們代禱

A Sigh of Remembrance

In some secluded spaces,
Some words cannot be spoken, deeds cannot be told.
History can only transform into a sigh in moments of remembrance,
mourning our fleeting and helpless lives within the confines of space.
The often-mentioned God's view is just an aspect of Rashomon,
cycling through the social progress of mankind.
And in our helpless frailty,
the spirit of the universe intercedes for us
with groanings too deep for words

詩 評
Review

這首詩以深刻的沉思捕捉了言語與行為的必然遺漏，歸結為歷史的沉默嘆息。使用「羅生門」來描繪觀點的多樣性，增強了對主觀真理和記憶的探索。

In a deeply contemplative tone, this poem captures the inevitability of unspoken words and untold deeds, resigning to history's silent sigh. The use of Rashomon to illustrate the multiplicity of perspectives enhances the poem's exploration of subjective truth and memory. It is a poignant reflection on the cycles of societal progress and individual impotence.

你我的星際

幻想唯美的一粒星塵漂浮
宇宙的天中 地球不斷的尋覓
當落日與月圓的球體終於懸掛東西
歲月猶如鳥鳴的春季
在你我的腦海中緩緩打開
即便 我們相處各自遙遠的星際

Our Interstellar Dream

Fantasy of delicate stardust drifting,
In the cosmos, the Earth ceaselessly seeks,
As the sun sets and the full moon hangs across the horizon,
Time unfolds like the chirping of birds in spring,
Slowly awakening in our minds.
Even though we dwell, each in distant stars of our own.

詩 評
Review

本詩捕捉了宇宙的壯麗和個體感知的親密性，將天體的宏偉舞蹈轉化為跨越想像與現實界限的個人敘事。

Capturing the grandeur of the cosmos and the intimacy of individual perception, this poem paints a picture of celestial beauty and personal yearning. It brings out the poetic grace in scientific wonder, turning the cosmic dance of planets and stars into a personal narrative that spans the bounds of imagination and reality.

家鄉的桃花紅了

在似有似無的春天的飄散裡
城市的輪廓漸隱風中
味道是最柔遠的撫摸
一壇醉生夢死迴響沉默
撥動無處安放的心弦
你坐在窗口眺望
時光凝聚成歲月的淚痕

家鄉的桃花紅了
遙遠的遐思在四月的紐約
瀰漫成羅斯福島櫻花的粉塵漫舞
收回我想像的風箏
一壺清茶在吉他的詠嘆中的瀑布
遠山綿延的近處
後院的野草地繁茂著桃花一株

The Peach Blossoms of My Hometown Are in Bloom

In the faint dispersal of an elusive spring,
the city's silhouette gradually fades into the wind.
The scent is the softest caress,
a jar of dreams and silence echoing,
stirring the restless strings of the heart.
You sit by the window, gazing out,
as time solidifies into the teardrops of the years.

The peach blossoms of my hometown are in bloom.
Distant musings in April's New York
spread into a dance of cherry blossom dust on Roosevelt Island.
I reel in my imaginary kite,
a pot of green tea cascades like a waterfall with the serenade of a guitar.
Near the distant mountains,
in the lush wild grass of the backyard, a single peach tree thrives.

詩 評
Review

這首詩以生動的桃花意象鮮明地捕捉了懷舊情緒的本質。它將個人的懷念情感與更廣闊的時間背景交織在一起，表達了時代懷舊與落葉歸根的主題。

This poem vibrantly captures the essence of nostalgia through the vivid imagery of peach blossoms. It juxtaposes the personal sentiment of longing and the broader strokes of time, bringing out a universal theme of returning to one's roots. The sensory details enrich the tapestry of memory, making the hometown a vivid character in its own right.

四月的日子

春天的風撫摸出嫩綠
楊柳枝頭籠罩團團青煙
紅楓花盛開著簇狀紅色的細鬚
灑滿哈德遜河谷的紐約鄉下
黛色的遠山在窗外的細雨中遙望
夕光穿過鄉鎮主街的舊日繁花
在古董店的一隅回憶已逝的容顏
從三百年的木橋走過
瞬間回憶起「又見炊煙」的歌曲
那是1980年的北京
在我心中雕刻的記憶

Days of April

Spring's breeze coaxes out tender greens,
Willow branches shroud in wisps of green mist,
Red maple flowers bloom with clusters of fine crimson tendrils,
Sprawling across the countryside of New York's Hudson Valley.
Indigo mountains gaze from beyond the window in a light drizzle,
Evening light filters through the old blossoms of the town's main street,
In a corner of the antique shop, memories of vanished faces linger,
Crossing over a three-hundred-year-old wooden bridge,
In an instant, I recall the song "Once Again I See the Cooking Smoke",
That is Beijing of 1980,
Carved into the memories of my heart.

詩 評
Review

這首詩以春天的細膩描繪框架了一幅跨越地域與時代的情感畫卷。詩中提到的「紐約哈德遜河谷的春光」與「1980年北京的舊影」之間的對比，不僅是景觀上的切換，更是情感記憶的流動與迴響。巧妙連結了紐約春天的景色及詩人對北京青春時光的懷念。

透過將鄧麗君的《又見炊煙》這首充滿懷舊色彩的歌曲融入詩句，詩人巧妙地觸發了讀者對於個人過去美好時光的共鳴，這種懷舊的情感特別適合表達對一個時代以及與之相關的人和事的深情回顧。詩中春天的生動描繪與個人回憶的交織，不僅展現了自然景觀的美麗，也觸動了深藏心中的情感。這種時空跨度的創作手法，讓這首詩充滿了深刻的情感共鳴和文化的豐富性。

This poem delicately frames spring to paint an emotional canvas that transcends both geography and time. The contrast between the "spring light in New York's Hudson Valley" and "the old shadows of Beijing in 1980" is more than a shift in scenery—it's a flow and echo of emotional memory. It cleverly connects the landscapes of spring in New York with the poet's nostalgic recollections of youth in Beijing.

By integrating Teresa Teng's nostalgic song "Once Again I See the Mist of Smoke" into the verse, the poet skillfully resonates with the readers' memories of their own pasts. This nostalgic emotion is particularly suited for reflecting deeply on an era and its related people and events. The vivid depiction of spring and the interweaving of personal memories showcase the beauty of natural landscapes and touch deep-seated emotions. This cross-temporal creative approach fills the poem with profound emotional resonance and cultural richness.

遠山三重奏

喜愛看遠山起伏的輪廓
那一抹雲煙深遠的黛色
漂浮在暮冬染黃枯枝的山脊
展現著被春喚醒的層茸茸青澀
三月的紅楓花在萬山叢林的枝頭
展開毛絨絨的羽翼

山野開放出一片片迷離的紅霧
大雁的翅膀掠過清澈的野湖
親愛的問候從萬裡的京城飄來
如同那遠山無聲的呼喚
安慰了我遠眺家鄉的心情

Distant Mountain Trio

I love to gaze at the undulating contours of distant mountains,
A hint of deep indigo mist,
Floating above the ridges with branches yellowed by late winter,
Displaying the verdant fuzziness awakened by spring.
In March, the red maple flowers
Spread their fluffy wings on the branches across myriad mountains.

The wilds release a hazy red mist,
As swan wings sweep across the crystal-clear wilderness lake.
Greetings drift from thousands miles of distant capital,
Like the silent call of those far mountains,
Soothing my longing heart as I gaze towards home.

詩 評
Review

本詩以強烈的意象和情感深度捕捉了自然景觀及其對人類精神的影響，是對嚮往與歸屬感的抒情探索。

詩中描繪的遠山不僅是自然的一部分，更像徵深遠的思念與情感的迴響。透過"那一抹雲煙深遠的黛色"與"漂浮在暮冬染黃枯枝的山脊"，詩人以畫家的筆觸捕捉了季節交替的瞬間美景，將個人的情感景觀與廣闊的自然景觀巧妙地連接起來，透過遙望山野的視角，表達了詩人對家鄉的懷念與心靈的慰藉。

This poem captures the natural landscape and its impact on the human spirit with vivid imagery and profound emotional depth, exploring themes of longing and belonging.

The distant mountains depicted are not merely elements of nature but also symbols of deep nostalgia and emotional resonance. Through phrases like "the deep indigo mist" and "branches yellowed by late winter," the poet employs a painterly touch to capture the fleeting beauty of changing seasons, skillfully bridging personal emotional landscapes with the vast natural scenery. By gazing through the mountains, the poet articulates a deep yearning for and solace in thoughts of hometown, intertwining the personal with the universal in a poignant reflection.

四月的紀念

四月的暖風緩緩掠過身邊
新綠的氣息若宛綿綿細雨的詩行
紐約鄉下的一株桃花悄然綻放
釋出冬日遺留的幾許倉皇

城市的街道洋溢著車水馬龍的輕快
冬的沉寂被無聲的春歌取代
臉上的微笑像四月無翼的使者，
八重櫻怒放的枝頭沉甸甸綴滿希望

在復甦的季節寫下對你的思念
未曾寄出的信也盛滿野花的清新
四月的星空閃爍著你我曾許下的諾言
靜夜中獨自一人聽著當年心跳的回音

April's Remembrance

The warm breeze of April gently sweeps by,
The scent of new greenery like a poem of soft drizzle.
A peach blossom in New York countryside quietly unfurls,
Releasing the remnants of winter's haste.

The city streets are bustling with lively traffic,
The silence of winter replaced by the silent songs of spring.
Smiles on faces like April's wingless messengers,
Branches of double cherry blossoms heavily laden with hope.

In this reviving season, I pen my longing for you,
Letters never sent, now brimming with the freshness of wildflowers.
April's starry sky twinkles with promises we once made,
Alone in the quiet night, I listen to the echoes of past heartbeats.

詩 評
Review

這首詩透過細膩、短暫的意象，美妙地捕捉了春天瞬間的片段及其與個人記憶的共鳴，反思了自然的變革力量及其喚起的深刻個人思考。

Filled with delicate, ephemeral imagery, this poem beautifully captures the fleeting moments of spring and their resonance with personal memories. It reflects on the transformational power of nature and its capacity to evoke deep, personal reflections about love, loss, and the passage of time.

四月的靈魂

四月在光影中與靈魂漫舞
緩緩綻放時間的繁花
每一瓣開放著對宇宙的訴說，
每一次呼吸著星際的塵埃

粉桃無言地綻放著燦爛的愛
每一朵來自靈魂深處的花開
四月的雨滴在天空中晶瑩低語
彼岸的呼喚幻化成水中的漣漪

靈魂的生命如同這勃發的時節，
萬物感受到存在的奇蹟
每一個生命都承載著宇宙的內在
在此世的旅程上煥發著潛在的靈性

April Spirit

April dances with the spirit amidst light and shadow,
Slowly unfurling the blossoms of time.
Each petal opens, telling tales of the cosmos,
Each breath inhaling the dust of the stars.

The blush of peach blossoms silently radiates splendid love,
Each bloom emerging from the depths of the soul.
April's raindrops whisper crystalline in the sky,
The call from beyond transforms into ripples upon the water.

The life of the spirit is like this burgeoning season,
All things feel the miracle of existence.
Every life bears the universe within,
Radiating its latent spirituality on this earthly journey.

詩 評
Review

詩中探討了更新和精神重生的主題，封裝了春天變革力量的本質。每一行都充滿了生命力，將自然的重生與更深層、幾乎神秘的靈魂更新聯繫起來。

The poem dances with themes of renewal and spiritual rebirth, encapsulating the essence of spring's transformative power. Each line thrums with life, tying the rebirth of nature to a deeper, almost mystical renewal of the soul, offering a reflective and uplifting perspective on the season.

輪迴

在此生的輪迴中 我們再次相遇，
彼岸的前世是我們此岸的倒影
你的眼眸藏著千禧年的秘密，
我的心跳迴盪著萬年的樂曲

穿越了時間的長河與無數的生命
我們總在尋找彼此的蹤跡
每一次遇見是命中看不見的注定
每一次別離都布下了來世重逢的根基

在塵世的角落 我們無數次相擁
前世的誓約纏綿訴說至今生
你的笑容，是我穿越千年的渴望
我的牽手，是你萬年回眸的承諾

時光的流轉編織著永恆的傳說
所有的遇見都不是偶然
星月流轉的生生世世彼此相依
在高緯的俯瞰 塵世繁花盡散

Reincarnation

In this life's cycle, we meet again,
The past lives from the other side are reflections of our present.
Your eyes hold secrets of a thousand years,
My heartbeat echoes melodies of ten thousand.

Through the long river of time and countless lives,
We always seek each other's traces.
Every encounter is an invisible destiny,
Every departure lays the foundation for a future reunion.

In the corners of the mortal world, we embrace countless times,
The vows of past lives linger and speak into this life.
Your smile is my longing through the millennia,
My handholding is your promise of a thousand-year return.

The flow of time weaves eternal legends,
All meetings are not by chance.
Through eons, under star and moon, we depend on each other,
From a high latitude, all the worldly blooms scatter.

詩 評
Review

這首詩提供了對精神連續性的深刻探討，將過去和現在的生活編織成一個永恆的整體。豐富的意象顯示了命運和命運的複雜舞蹈，超越了時間，體現了永恆回歸和精神相互聯繫的主題。

This piece offers a profound exploration of spiritual continuity, weaving past and present lives into a single, eternal tapestry. The imagery is rich and layered, suggesting an intricate dance of fate and destiny that transcends time, embodying the poem's theme of eternal return and spiritual interconnectedness.

光影中的塵埃

走在蒙哥馬利的小徑上
聽見宇宙呼吸的寂寥在草地上迴響
來自遠處的斑駁光影達成的棚帳
越過屋脊 穿過樹叢的透射
而我就像一粒輕舞的塵埃
夕光中隨著夕陽的遠去飛揚

你我都是地球上一粒微小的星塵
任憑宇宙的力量在身邊飛速流淌
想起小時候仰望星空的幻想
那夢想中的光影騎士和超人
無形地傳輸著千百年時間線的縱橫
那造物主掌控人類命運的能量

光影的橘色在遠山深處飄揚
精神碰撞時隱時現轉換的模樣
宇宙時空的漫天星辰是你留下的腳印
與我偶遇後凝固住的時光
覺醒如同地球輪迴不息的篇章，
眺望一望無際中流星墜落的光芒

Dust in the Light and Shadow

Walking on a path in Montgomery,
I hear the lonely breath of the universe echoing over the grass.
Patchy light and shadows create a canopy,
Crossing rooftops, filtering through the trees,
And I, like a dancing speck of dust,
Flutter away with the setting sun in the evening light.

You and I are mere specks of stardust on Earth,
Subject to the swift flow of cosmic forces around us.
I recall childhood fantasies gazing up at the starry sky,
Dreaming of knights of light and superheroes,
Silently transmitting through timelines of centuries,
The Creator's energy that shapes human destiny.

The orange hues of light and shadow flutter in the distant mountains,
Our spirits appear and vanish, shifting forms in collision.
The vast universe's stars are the footprints you leave behind,
Solidifying the moment after we meet.
Awakening, like Earth's unceasing cycle,
I gaze at the endless sky, watching meteors fall in radiant streams.

詩 評
Review

這首詩捕捉了生命短暫性對廣闊宇宙背景的感慨。它以抒情和內省的方式展示了人類存在的短暫性，描繪了生命如同在光影中舞動的塵埃，但又深受宇宙連結的影響。

This poem captures the ephemeral quality of life against the backdrop of the cosmos. It presents a lyrical and introspective look at human existence, portraying life as transient dust caught in the vast play of light and shadow yet underscored by a deep cosmic connection.

通靈的能力

你說 人類喪失了通靈的能力
物質的眼睛已經覆蓋地球
藝術也不再隨心所欲
每個人都在尋找老師學習
卻忽略了自身內在的能力
形式上的複製代代相傳
看不見軀殼裡精神正壓抑地呼吸

傾聽內心的呼聲
給靈魂舒展時空的氣力
被遺忘的夢中喚醒失落的自己
每個生命都有自我的軌跡
如同風中浪漫的落英
看得見惜香的遺憾
看不見世代時光的更替

The Lost Art of Spirit Communication

You say humanity has lost the ability to communicate with spirits,
Material eyes have now covered the Earth,
Art no longer flows freely from the heart.
Everyone is looking for a teacher to learn from,
Ignoring the innate abilities within themselves.
The replication of forms is passed down through generations,
Unseen, the spirit within struggles to breathe.

Listen to the call of your heart,
Give your soul the space and energy to stretch,
Awaken the forgotten self in dreams left behind.
Every life follows its own unique path,
Like petals romantically scattered by the wind,
Visible are the regrets of lost fragrance,
Invisible, the relentless passage of time through generations.

詩 評
Review

透過沉思的語調，這首詩批評了現代對精神和藝術直覺的脫節，哀嘆了本能能力的喪失，這些能力被物質觀點和形式教育所取代，呼籲重新與內在聲音聯繫，這是對複製世界中真實性的懇求。

Through its meditative tone, the poem critiques modern disconnection from spiritual and artistic intuition. It laments the loss of innate abilities, overridden by materialistic views and formal education, calling for a reconnection with the inner voice—a plea for authenticity in a replicated world.

三層死亡

在塵世的一角，墓地的邊緣
每人都會經歷一次死亡
生命的暗影在終點的時刻
會沉默地等在身旁
無論你我都難以逃亡

看不見的彼岸無形的界限
玻璃瓶裡逃亡生命的沙漏
消失的悼詞如宇宙的顫動
萬物終究歸宿於無形
甚至 沒有人記得你曾經來過

記憶輕輕劃過時間的表層
直到名字最終溶於虛無
光影流轉的脆弱終於將你淹沒
世界上再也聽不到曾經的音訊
儘管那是你曾經存在的全部

死亡是終極意義上的淪喪
生理的死亡流於形式上的悲傷
當最終的遺忘來臨時
世界早已不記得軀殼的存在
只有曾經的愛雕刻心上

Three Tiers of Death

In a corner of this mortal world, at the edge of a graveyard,
Every person will experience death once.
The shadow of life waits silently at the side
At the moment of termination,
Neither you nor I can escape.

The invisible shore has unseen boundaries,
Life's hourglass flees within a glass bottle,
Vanishing eulogies tremble like the universe,
All things ultimately return to the intangible,
Even no one remembers you were ever here.

Memory gently skims the surface of time,
Until names finally dissolve into nothingness,
The fragile flow of light and shadow eventually engulfs you,
No longer can the world hear any news of the past,
Though that was all of your existence.

Death is the ultimate loss of meaning,
Physiological death turns into mere formal sorrow.
When the final oblivion arrives,
The world has already forgotten the existence of the shell,
Only the love once carved in the heart remains.

詩 評
Review

這首詩深入探討了死亡的存在層面，探索了其不可避免性及伴隨的孤獨。生命如暫時的陰影掠過時間，捕捉了存在的短暫性，提供了對生命終點和遺忘的沉思。

This poignant poem delves into the existential layers of death, exploring its inevitability and the solitude that accompanies it. The imagery of life as a fleeting shadow over time captures the transient nature of existence, offering a somber yet profound reflection on the finality of life and the forgetfulness of death.

晚思

夕光的透視穿越茶室的空間
橘色的影子詭異地流離失所
那色正好 灑滿瑰麗的盛宴
窗外的雲影遮住了斜陽
我在暗中觀望
任憑暮色的流水漸漸滲透
那一抹晚霞漂浮的遐想
春的聲音被隱晦隔離在遙遠
只剩下一點點紫紅的雲煙
抹在沉默的記憶和天邊

Evening Thoughts

Evening light's perspective pierces through the teahouse space,
Orange shadows eerily drift,
Just the right hue, spilling over a magnificent feast.
Cloud shadows outside the window obscure the evening light,
I observe in the shadows,
Allowing the hues of dusk to gradually permeate.
These hints of twilight spark drifting daydreams,
The voice of spring is muted and distant in the dimness,
Only bits of purple-red cloud smoke
Painted across silent memories and the horizon.

詩 評
Review

這首詩平靜而又帶有鬼魅的反思,捕捉了黃昏時光光與影的交互作用。它將自然和城市的意象融合,反思生命短暫時刻的寧靜和複雜性。

A tranquil yet haunting reflection on the interplay of light and shadows during dusk, this poem captures the quiet beauty and the introspective mood of evenings. It blends natural and urban imagery to reflect on the transient moments of life, encapsulating the serene yet complex nature of twilight musings.

迷月

無論一輪圓的豐滿還是優雅半彎
愛你樹梢後的若隱若現
像是一團裊裊升起的迷霧
在被暗夜沉寂的心湖投擲
水中一道隱約的光泉

曾經 月是嫦娥思念吳剛的夢幻
孤獨中多少次抬頭仰望
期待有情人的最終團圓
屋脊上的月影在幽暗的時空中
卻刻入時代顛沛流離失所的歲月

曾幾何時 月是枕水江南的雲煙
飄散在石橋下篷船水鄉的邊緣
那些失落的日子像一本筆記
在風中翻飛出曾畫過的才子佳人
年輕歲月只是浩瀚宇宙中的一點兒

穿過滄海的原野與桑田的遠山
你依然飛翔在遙不可及的遠天
像一輪永遠猜不透的山水謎團
在鏡花水月的薄紗後照見
每人前世今生的命運之輪

Enchanted Moon

Whether full and plump or a graceful crescent,
I love your elusive presence behind the treetops,
Like a wisp of mist rising,
Cast into the still lake of a night-darkened heart,
A faint glow springs from the water.

Once, the moon was Chang'e's dreamy longing for Wu Gang,
How many times have I looked up in solitude,
Hoping for the ultimate reunion of lovers,
The moon's shadow on the roof, in the dim expanse of time,
Yet engraved with the tumultuous years of an era.

There was a time when the moon was the mist over water-town Jiangnan,
Drifting at the edge of stone bridges and boat-strewn waterways,
Those lost days are like a notebook,
Flipping in the wind, revealing scholars and beauties once sketched,
Youth but a mere speck in the vast universe.

Crossing the wilderness of the sea and the distant mountains of the past,
You still soar in the unreachable distant sky,
Like an eternally enigmatic landscape riddle,
Seen through the gauzy veil of mirrored flowers and water,
Reflecting the wheel of fate of each person's past and present lives.

詩 評
Review

這首詩透過豐富的神話和情感深度，編織了月亮對人情感和時間流逝的影響。使用天體比喻深入探討了渴望、記憶和生命與愛的永恆循環。

Rich in mythology and emotion, this poem weaves lunar imagery with personal reflection. It explores the moon's influence over human feelings and the passage of time, using celestial metaphors to delve into themes of longing, memory, and the eternal cycle of life and love.

語言的塊狀理解

時間與空間以像素的形態存在
於是 光形成的撫摸
粒子的能量快速衝破
想像是一種張力
被藝術的語言俘獲
在2024年的第二個早晨
或許是宇宙無數個星晨
我所看到的 是否
你眼中的內在光波
彩虹的光道形成的凱旋
世上只有些人用生命探索
所有的人懂與不懂
都無所謂的理解
生命只是一道水紋形成的力量
如同沙灘的遙遠的平滑
近看時卻是一顆顆沙礫
形成的起伏
我們的生命都在此刻相遇
此刻即是永恆

Understanding of Language in Cubes

Time and space exist in the form of pixels,
Thus, light forms a caress,
The energy of particles swiftly breaks through.
Imagination is a form of tension,
Captured by the language of art.
On the second morning of 2024,
Or perhaps on one of the countless starry mornings of the universe,
What I see, is it
the inner light waves in your eyes?
The triumphant path formed by the rainbow's light,
Only some people explore with their lives,
Understanding, whether comprehensible to all or none,
Does not truly matter.
Life is merely a force formed by a ripple on water,
Like the distant smoothness of a sandy area,
Yet, up close, it is grains of sand,
Forming undulations.
Our lives meet at this moment,
This moment is an eternity.

詩 評
Review

探索時間和空間作為可知構造的抽象概念，這首詩哲學地從事對感知、現實和存在的概念的思考。它反思了人類理解的限制和可能性，透過生命如過水波紋的比喻，沉思了存在的宇宙尺度。

This poem philosophically engages with concepts of perception, reality, and existence, exploring the abstraction of time and space as perceivable constructs. It reflects on the limitations and possibilities of human understanding, contemplating the cosmic scale of existence through the metaphor of life as transient water ripples.

天空是一片懸浮的宇宙

夢中
天空是一片懸浮的宇宙
一團團飄搖著
世間的憂愁
天際裂縫的深處
倒掛的城市天際線
旋轉又旋轉著
彷彿失去引力的迷城
在紅色的夕光中
有著迷人的機械的轉動

看一團團的漂浮物
在天的深處慢慢遙遠
被拋棄的物品家具書本
甚至紅色的衣物
緩緩飄向光的深處
消失成黑色的陰影團團

忽然又見窗外
樹杈上匐匍的一隻隻鴿子
灰紅色的翅膀
夕陽映照出斑駁的光影
彷彿動物園的展示廳
清澈的玻璃與我相隔一層
我在看你 誰在看我？

一次次醒來又睡去
依然是同一個夢的宇宙
同樣的飄搖與懸浮
夕光匯成風浩瀚的紅海
充滿天際的溫柔想像
我伸手去觸摸
永遠停不下的漂浮物
卻忽然感到渺小

The Sky is a Suspended Universe

In dreams,
the sky is a suspended universe,
swirling clusters
of worldly sorrows.
Deep within the cracks of the horizon,
a city skyline hangs upside down,
spinning and spinning,
like a lost city devoid of gravity,
in the red glow of the evening,
enchanted by the mechanical turning.

Floating orbs are seen,
drifting into the depths of the sky, slowly and distantly,
discarded items, furniture, books,
even red garments,
gently float toward the deep light,
vanishing into black shadowy clusters.

Suddenly, outside the window,
a pigeon creeps along a tree branch,
its gray-red wings
casting mottled shadows in the sunset,
resembling a display in a zoo.
A clear glass separates us,
I am watching you; who is watching me?

Waking and sleeping again and again,
still in the same dream universe,
the same swaying and suspension,
evening light merging into a vast red sea of wind,
filled with tender imaginings of the horizon.
I reach out to touch
the endlessly drifting objects,
yet suddenly feel minuscule,

似一粒灰燼與塵土
再次醒來時
新鮮的陽光從雲的縫隙中
將悶熱的日子撕扯

like a speck of ash and dust.
When I wake again,
fresh sunlight tears through the gaps in the clouds,
rending the stifling days.

詩 評
Review

這首詩以夢幻般的超現實主義捕捉了想像力的無限性，將日常生活與宇宙相對比。透過懸浮宇宙的意象挑戰了現實感知，喚起了對無限和夢境內含界限的感知。

Dreamlike and surreal, this poem captures the boundlessness of the imagination, juxtaposing the everyday with the cosmic. The imagery of a suspended universe over mundane life challenges perceptions of reality, invoking a sense of wonder and the infinite within the confines of the dream world.

秋夢乍醒

我站在高樓的頂端
舉著我的蘋果手機
一位年長的陌生男人
坐在樓頂的左邊
我眺望著遠方的風景
灰藍色雲層深疊出的時空下
黑色樓宇的屋脊起伏綿延
彷彿曼哈頓的天際線
又彷彿建築古老的江南
黑色的剪影以最遼闊的姿態
舒展角樓 古塔 廟堂的盤旋
在黃昏即逝 夜幕將至的瞬間
我被這難以言述的景緻擊中內心

如同往常的拍攝
聚焦的鏡頭中逐漸清晰著樓宇
漸漸呈現的紅色流彩著閃爍的黑金
古老的歷史浮雕忽然
逸動著高緯的影像
光頭的男人在釋放著
一隻展翅欲飛的鳥兒
金色的亮光取代了黑金的暗光
我的驚訝被凝固成視野裡的奇幻
在鏡頭的移動中
近景裡的活動讓我不斷按下快門

忽然一切遠遁 時光轉瞬
睜開眼睛 哲學貓睡在身邊
夢的鏡子居然如此清晰
折射出超越想像的壯麗無限
我在秋天的早晨開車出門
驚見路邊一棵樹黑色的枝椏
盛開著朵朵白玉蘭
盛秋的十月開以春天的姿態

Autumn Dream, Suddenly Awakened

I stand at the top of a skyscraper,
holding my iPhone,
a senior stranger sits to the left on the rooftop.
I gaze into the distance,
beneath a sky of layered gray-blue clouds,
the undulating rooftops of black buildings stretch out,
reminiscent of Manhattan's skyline,
and yet, akin to the ancient architecture of Jiangnan.
The black silhouettes expansively unfold,
spiraling around pagodas, ancient towers, and temples.
In the fleeting twilight, as night approaches,
I am struck by this indescribable vista.
As usual in my photography,
the focused lens gradually clarifies the buildings,
unveiling a shimmering black and gold with red hues.

Suddenly, an ancient historical bas-relief
springs to life with high-latitude imagery.
A bald man releases
a bird poised for flight.
Golden light replaces the dark luster of black gold,
my astonishment frozen into the fantastical view in my sight.

As the camera moves,
the foreground activity prompts me to press the shutter continually.
Suddenly, everything recedes, time flashes by,
I open my eyes, and the philosophical cat sleeps beside me.
The mirror of dreams was so vivid,
reflecting a splendor beyond imagination.
As I drive out on an autumn morning,
I am startled to see a roadside tree with black branches,
blooming with clusters of white magnolias,
in an October as vibrant as spring,
conveying messages from cosmic angels.

傳達著來自宇宙天使的訊息
正如你說 時間可以看見
虛無以看得見的實體
投擲在信者的心間

Just as you said, time can be seen,
nothingness materialized,
cast into the hearts of believers.

詩 評
Review

將夢境的生動性與現實的鮮明對比，這首詩探討了想像與現實之間的微妙界線。透過動態的意象捕捉了突然清晰的時刻，這些時刻在心靈的眼中凝固，提供了對感知和存在性質的深刻反思。

Blending the vividness of dreams with the starkness of reality, this poem explores the thin line between the imagined and the real. It uses dynamic imagery to capture moments of sudden clarity, where the beauty and complexity of life are crystallized in the mind's eye, offering a deep, reflective pause on the nature of perception and existence.

遠方無聲鴿

穿過懼風雨停息的瞬間
云如旗幟飄揚在遠山
寂靜覆蓋山的野徑
記憶的水珠滯留在落葉的背面
遠方的鴿子煽動的翅膀
穿過千百年的世紀
掀起靈與靈的對話

A Dove on Distant Oaks

Through the moment when storms cease,
Clouds flutter like flags over distant mountains.
Silence envelops the wild paths of the mountain,
Droplets of memory cling to the underside of fallen leaves.
The distant dove, with its flapping wings,
Crosses centuries,
Stirring a dialogue between spirits.

詩 評
Review

《遠方無聲鴿》是一首充滿象徵意義與深刻感悟的詩篇。詩人透過描繪一幅寧靜的自然景觀——風暴過後的寧靜、遠山上飄揚的雲朵和沈寂的山徑，引入了一隻遙遠的鴿子，象徵著時間的深遠和靈魂的溝通。這隻鴿子與其翅膀的輕拍不僅穿越了物理的距離，也連結了歷史的長河，掀起了跨越時空的精神對話。這首詩以其深邃的內涵和精緻的意象，展現了詩人對生命和宇宙連結的獨到見解。

"A Dove on Distant Oaks" is a poem rich in symbolism and profound insights. The poet crafts a serene natural scene—post-storm tranquility, clouds billowing over distant mountains, and silent mountain paths—to introduce a distant dove, symbolizing the depths of time and spiritual communication. The dove's gentle flapping not only traverses physical distances but also bridges historical epochs, initiating a dialogue across time and spirit. With its profound connotations and exquisite imagery, the poem presents the poet's unique perspective on the connections between life and the cosmos.

作者後記

這本詩集裡的十九首詩歌都是2024年的近作，闡述了我靈魂的看見。之所以說靈魂，是因為這些詩歌全都是瞬間想法的結晶，　表達了精神層面的感知和感悟，　看上去似乎與我們每日的生活無關，但對我自己來說卻至關重要。　或許我就是一個為靈魂而活著的人，常常感知感覺不到物質層面的需求，而是靈魂自由自在的飛翔。

好在我住的紐約上州的鄉下遠離城市和喧囂，有大自然的環境給我提供了春夏秋冬四個季節變換時的廣袤、寂靜、空曠和深遠，從日出到日落都能夠給我帶來精神上的歡愉。

在這樣環境中寫成的詩歌，不僅僅是停留在對大自然的感知上，而是超越了時間與空間地眺望無限星空，探索我們的靈魂來源與歸處。

感謝當代科技AI的誕生，詩歌翻譯和評論不再是一個難題。　我邀請AI擔任了這本詩集的英文翻譯助理，及中英文詩歌評論撰寫，讓這本詩集的內容更加豐富。　我覺得儘管AI不具備人的情感，但卻具有超越人類的智能。尤其，AI根據它所擁有的大數據來評價一首詩歌時，具有博覽群書的經驗及更高的視野，使詩歌評論摒棄私心雜念，更為公正，這也是我邀請AI參與的目的。

Author's Afterword

The nineteen poems in this collection are recent works from 2024, elucidating the visions of my soul. I refer to the soul because these poems are crystallizations of spontaneous thoughts, expressing perceptions and insights on a spiritual level that may seem unrelated to our everyday lives, yet are of utmost importance to me. Perhaps I am someone who lives for the soul, often oblivious to material needs, allowing my spirit the freedom to soar.

Fortunately, I reside in the countryside of Upstate New York, far from the city's hustle and bustle. The natural environment here provides vastness, silence, openness, and depth through the changing seasons from spring to winter, bringing me spiritual joy from sunrise to sunset.

The poems written in such an environment are not merely about sensing nature but transcend time and space, gazing into the infinite starry sky, and exploring the origins and destinations of our souls.

Thanks to the advent of contemporary AI technology, translating poetry and writing critiques is no longer a daunting task. I have enlisted AI to handle the English translation as my assistant and to write poetry reviews in both Chinese and English, enriching the content of this collection. I believe that although AI lacks human emotions, it possesses intelligence that often surpasses human capabilities in many aspects. Especially when AI evaluates a poem based on the vast data it has access to, it draws from a breadth of literature and a higher perspective, ensuring its critiques are devoid of personal bias, thus more impartial. This is why I invited AI to participate.

胡桃，筆名紐約桃花，資深節目製片、作家及出版人。她曾為中國中央電視台、CBS和MTV，擔任助理節目編導及製片。1980年代，胡桃開始為《外國戲劇》和《讀者文摘》等雜誌撰稿，並成為中國女記者協會會員。1990年代初，她從布魯克林學院獲得電視製作與廣播新聞碩士學位，並曾在CBS擔任節目翻譯。1994年至1995年，她開始在美國音樂電視台MTV工作，並為MTV亞洲部的三個音樂電視節目担任制片人，創立了中國大陸首個非常受歡迎的音樂頻道《天籟村》。2019年，她創立了美國龍出版社，擔任出版人。2024年11月，她製作的短篇紀錄片《From Stone to Stone》獲得柏林獨立電影節獲最佳短片導演獎。

自2015年以來，胡桃在美國、中國和台灣的中文雜誌及報紙上發表非虛構文章、詩歌和小說，多次獲得文學獎的首獎和優秀獎。她所撰寫的家族歷史傳記文學《上海浮生若夢》和非虛構文集《往事經年流水夢》分別在2022年獲得「首屆海外華人影視文學」優秀創意獎，及2023年「海外華文著述獎」新聞報道首獎。

Sonia Hu, known by her pen name Niu Yue Tao Hua, is an esteemed program producer, writer, and publisher. Starting her career as an assistant director and producer for networks like CCTV (China Central Television Network), CBS, and MTV, she ventured into writing in the 1980s with works featured in magazines like Foreign Drama and Reader's Digest. Sonia became a member of the Chinese Women Journalists Association. She graduated with a master's degree in television production and broadcasting journalism from Brooklyn College in the early 1990s. During 1994-1995, at MTV Music Network, she produced three daily music television programs for MTV Asia and established Mainland China's first popular music channel, "Village of Heavenly Sound." In 2019, she founded Long Publishing Corp., continuing as its publisher. Her documentary From Stone to Stone won the Best Short Film Director Award at the Berlin Independent Film Festival in November 2024.

Sonia has been actively publishing nonfiction articles, poetry, and novels in Chinese newspapers and magazines across the United States, China, and Taiwan since 2015. Her works have repeatedly garnered top awards in literary contests. Her biographical literature, Shanghai Forever Lost, and nonfiction collection, Reminiscence of Fleeting Time, received the inaugural Excellent Creative Award for Overseas Chinese Film and Television Literature in 2022 and the top prize at the Overseas Chinese Literary Awards in 2023, respectively.

Reverie: A Collection of Poems
幻想詩集

Published by Long Publishing Corp.
A New York-based independent publisher
www.longpublisher.com

ISBN: 978-1-953903-13-6

Printed in the United States
First Edition: December 2024